BROKEN RECORDS

ADVENTURE RECORDS

TO GET YOUR HEART RACING!

KENNY ABDO

Fly!
An Imprint of Abdo Zoom
abdobooks.com

abdobooks.com

Published by Abdo Zoom, a division of ABDO, P.O. Box 398166, Minneapolis, Minnesota 55439.

Printed in the United States of America, North Mankato, Minnesota.
052023
092023

THIS BOOK CONTAINS RECYCLED MATERIALS

Photo Credits: Alamy, AP Images, Getty Images, Shutterstock, US Navy
Production Contributors: Kenny Abdo, Jennie Forsberg, Grace Hansen
Design Contributors: Candice Keimig, Neil Klinepier, Laura Graphenteen

Library of Congress Control Number: 2022946928

Publisher's Cataloging-in-Publication Data

Names: Abdo, Kenny, author.
Title: Adventure records to get your heart racing! / by Kenny Abdo
Description: Minneapolis, Minnesota : Abdo Zoom, 2024 | Series: Broken records | Includes online resources and index.
Identifiers: ISBN 9781098281366 (lib. bdg.) | ISBN 9781098282066 (ebook) | ISBN 9781098282417 (Read-to-me ebook)
Subjects: LCSH: Records--Juvenile literature. | History--Juvenile literature. | Adventure and adventurers--Juvenile literature.
Classification: DDC 032.02--dc23

TABLE OF CONTENTS

ADVENTURE RECORDS

Throughout history, people have looked for adventure. And by pushing themselves, humans have achieved world records along the way!

From long distance drives to **freefalling** from the Earth's **stratosphere**, these records will get anyone's heart racing!

BROKEN RECORDS

In 1888, Bertha Benz told her husband that she was going on a road trip. The drive was 66 miles (106 km) long. That made Benz the first person to drive an automobile over a long distance!

While in the **Royal Navy**, Poon Lim's ship was attacked in 1942. He survived 133 days alone at sea. Lim was picked up by a fishing boat in 1943. He earned the record for longest time spent surviving at sea on a life raft.

FELIX BAUMGARTNER

In 2012, Felix Baumgartner did a **freefall** jump from 24 miles (39 km) above Earth's surface. He attained the record for highest manned balloon flight, the fastest speed in freefall, and first human to break the **sound barrier**!

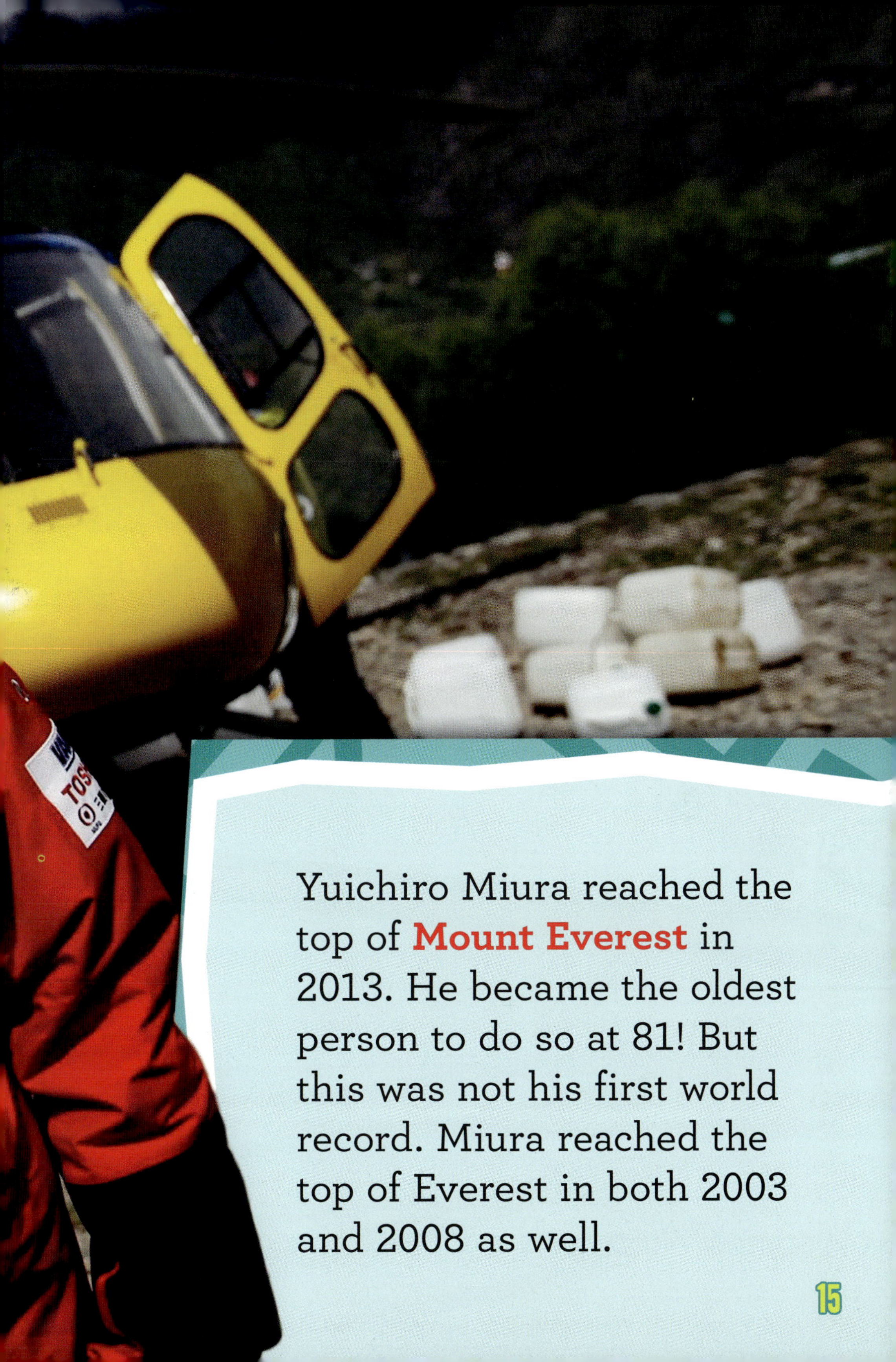

Yuichiro Miura reached the top of **Mount Everest** in 2013. He became the oldest person to do so at 81! But this was not his first world record. Miura reached the top of Everest in both 2003 and 2008 as well.

In 2018, Denise Mueller-Korenek wanted to see how fast bikes could really go. She rode a specialty bike hitched to a **dragster**. Mueller-Korenek set a new bike speed record of 183.9 mph (296 kmh), smashing the previous record of 167 mph (269 kmh)!

KHS
Project Speed
Fred Rompelberg
Bicycle Holidays
TE
PRIMAL
KHS
Bicycles Since 1975
Denise Korenek
Coach
John Howard
JOHN HOWARD
PERFORMANCE SPORTS
SECURITY BY
Rancho Santa Fe
SECURITY SYSTEMS
Fred Rompelberg
Bicycle Holidays
MALLORCA
U NATION
da Vinci

Surfer Sebastian Steudtner rode a 115-foot (35 m) wave in 2022. He surpassed the previous world record that he set himself, receiving a new **Guinness World Record** for the highest wave ever surfed!

FOR THE RECORD

For most adventurers, the journey matters more than the destination. But sometimes the journey ends with a world record!

GLOSSARY

dragster – a modified car built to perform in drag races.

freefall – the portion of skydiving when the parachute is not used.

Guinness World Record – an award given to those who have broken a record never achieved before.

Mount Everest – Earth's highest mountain that is above sea level. It is part of the Himalayan mountains, along the China and Nepal border.

Royal Navy – the United Kingdom's sea warfare force.

sound barrier – a sudden large increase in aerodynamic drag that occurs as the speed of an aircraft approaches the speed of sound.

stratosphere – a layer of the Earth's upper atmosphere from about six miles to about thirty miles above the earth's surface.

ONLINE RESOURCES

Booklinks
NONFICTION NETWORK
FREE! ONLINE NONFICTION RESOURCES

To learn more about adventure records, please visit **abdobooklinks.com** or scan this QR code. These links are routinely monitored and updated to provide the most current information available.

INDEX